Original title:
Beneath the Snow's Veil

Copyright © 2024 Creative Arts Management OÜ
All rights reserved.

Author: Samuel Kensington
ISBN HARDBACK: 978-9916-94-552-0
ISBN PAPERBACK: 978-9916-94-553-7

Beneath the Crystal Canopy

Squirrels in coats made for style,
Chasing snowflakes down the aisle.
Penguins in a silly dance,
Making winter's chill a chance.

Time Paused in Winter's Embrace

A snowman wearing shades so bright,
Dreaming of the warm sunlight.
Pine trees adorned in frosty bling,
Wonder what the spring will bring.

The Silence of Hidden Seasons

The rabbits plot their winter feast,
While frosty air will not be ceased.
Icicles hang like silly wigs,
On every house, as time just digs.

Where Warmth Dwells in Hibernation

Bears roll over in their dreams,
Knitting socks with utmost seams.
While mock snowflakes tickle their toes,
Spring will come, or so it goes.

The Quiet Language of Ice

Whispers of chill, a frosty rhyme,
Snowflakes giggle, keeping time.
A snowman dons his carrot nose,
While penguins slide, striking poses.

Icicles dangle, a sparkly show,
As kids in mittens try not to go slow.
They throw snowballs, with laughter loud,
A blizzard of fun in a winter crowd.

Shadows Dancing in White

In the moonlight, shadows prance,
A snowflake twirls, it takes a chance.
Snowmen try to break dance too,
But lose their heads—a funny view!

Creatures peek from behind the drift,
A little squirrel gives a gift.
He scurries on, his stash is blessed,
With nuts tucked safely in his nest.

The Secret Beneath the Frost

Under blankets cool and bright,
Squirrels plot their wild delight.
They hide their stash, oh what a prank,
A nutty treasure in a bank!

Winter's laughter, a comic flair,
With frozen toes, they dance in air.
Flip-flops lost in piles of white,
A fashion faux pas, what a sight!

The Lullaby of White Silence

A snowman dreams of warm sunshine,
While rabbits hop, they'll be just fine.
They chuckle low, in powder they play,
Whiskers twitching, they'll win the day.

Frosty nights hold secrets tight,
As winter's giggles bring delight.
A yawn escapes the sleeping trees,
They snore beneath the chilly breeze.

A Canvas Laid in Silence and Snow

A blanket of white on the ground,
With snowflakes dancing all around.
A squirrel slips, makes a funny face,
He thought he could fly, but lost his grace.

A snowman stands with a carrot nose,
But it wobbles; who knows how it goes?
His buttons are mismatched, oh what a sight,
He's more of a snow blob, try as he might.

Kids laugh while they stack, some fall with glee,
Creating a chaos, wild as can be.
They roll in the fluff, like little bears,
In a world of snowballs, laughter ensnares.

The trees wear coats, all frosty and bright,
You'd think they're ready for a snowball fight.
But they stand still, not one to engage,
Just giggle at whimsies, setting the stage.

The Hibernate Beneath the Chill

Squirrels in pajamas, cozy and snug,
Dreaming of acorns, giving a shrug.
Bears snooze away, plush as a cloud,
Snoring so loudly, they're drawing a crowd.

With blankets of white, they'll stay out of sight,
While winter plays tricks in the soft moonlight.
Counting their z's, no rush in this game,
What's better than napping? It's all the same!

Muted Colors in a Blanched World

Drab trees wear coats, just beige and gray,
No bright splashes here, it's a dull ballet.
Snowflakes are twirling, like they've lost their way,
Wonder where colors are? They've gone on holiday!

Frost-bitten bushes, they skip the bright hue,
They're all waiting patiently for spring's debut.
Whispers of blooms, they echo in dreams,
Hoping for sunlight to shatter the seams.

Secrets of the Frozen Ground

Under the frost lies a world of jest,
Rabbits tell tales of the very best.
Secret snowball fights in the dark of the night,
While the owls just hoot, "This isn't polite!"

Moles form a band with a concert of squeaks,
While the ice-coated critters play hide-and-seeks.
With giggles and whispers they dance in a trance,
Oh, to behold this chilly romance!

The Hidden Pulse of Winter

Tick-tock, tick-tock, winter's clock winks,
As penguins wear shades and dolphins think pinks.
Snowmen plot mischief, in scarves and hats,
Crafting warm cocoa with mischievous chats.

Icicles hang like a jester's long nose,
Twinkling with mischief, as everyone knows.
With snowballing giggles, they start a surprise,
'Tis the season of frozen fun in disguise!

Echoes of Nature's Soft Cloak

Squirrels don their winter coats,
Chasing nuts like tiny boats.
Penguins waddle, looking cool,
While rabbits dance around like fools.

The trees wear white, a playful guise,
As snowflakes fall from painted skies.
A snowman sports a carrot nose,
While nearby, a snowball slips and goes!

In the Thaw of Silent Slumber

As winter melts, the world gets bright,
Bunnies hop, full of delight.
The puddles form a bumpy stage,
Where frogs jump in a splashing rage.

But wait! What's that? A muddy shoe!
Oops, that's mine; I've slipped right through.
With laughter echoed all around,
I leap in joy—oh, what a sound!

Frosted Remnants of the Past

Last year's snowmen, stiff and gray,
Stand like statues, 'Do not play!'
But who could resist such frosty charms?
I take a chance; I roll my arms!

With one loud crash, they tumble down,
As giggles rise, not a single frown.
I swear I heard them say, 'Let's go!'
To find a hat and join the show!

Whispers in the Chill of the Air

The icicles dangle like sharp teeth,
As penguins slide in playful wreath.
Breezes giggle as they blow,
Whispers of secrets, just for show.

A snowball fight breaks out this morn,
Hit too hard, I twist and scorn.
"Oh no," I shout, "not my new gear!"
While laughter rings, I smile ear to ear!

The Dreams That Hide from Frost

In the nook where chit-chat's born,
Socks and mittens play all torn.
The snowman winks, he's not so grand,
But he's got plans, a snowy band.

The cat in boots, a swagger proud,
Chases snowflakes, oh so loud!
With each leap, a frosty cheer,
He thinks he's king, it's crystal clear.

Hot cocoa spills, the mug won't settle,
It dances like a bubbling kettle.
Dreams of summer tease the chill,
While frosty friends just sit and thrill.

When springtime teases from afar,
The snowmen ponder 'who's the star?'
With carrot noses, they debate,
Who plays the best in winter's fate.

A Tapestry Woven in Icy Threads

Lacy patterns on the ground,
In a world that spins around.
Each snowflake bears a silly face,
A frozen grin in every place.

The trees wear coats of glitter bright,
As squirrels bubble up in fright.
In winter's chill, they scurry fast,
Planning mischief, unsurpassed.

A snowball flies, the laughter roars,
And suddenly, we're all outdoors.
With frosty noses, hearts so bold,
The tales of winter never old.

As night descends, the stars will wink,
Underneath the moon's soft pink.
We weave together, threads of fun,
Chasing dreams till day is done.

Fragments of Life Beneath the Chill

A penguin slides, a clumsy show,
He wobbles left, then leaps to go.
In frozen lands, they've found a plot,
A dance-off where the air is hot!

The owls gossip, quite refined,
With tales of snowflakes, one of a kind.
They chuckle at the blingy frost,
With icy jewels, they are embossed.

The snowdrops peek, so brave, so bold,
Like tiny gems, they break the cold.
They giggle soft at winter's might,
And sing of spring with sheer delight.

As we dive into the snow so deep,
With laughter loud, and smiles we keep.
Each flake a puzzle, each frost a grin,
In chilly realms where fun begins.

Melodies of Nature's Winter Sleep

In a blanket soft and white,
The world prepares to sleep at night.
With muffled sounds, the giggles fade,
As winter paints its frosty parade.

The rabbits hop, wearing hats so grand,
Building castles in the icy sand.
The moonlight glimmers on their trails,
As laughter echoes through the gales.

Old man winter hums a tune,
While twinkling stars dance 'round the moon.
The trees sway gently, joining in,
With every note, they laugh and spin.

And as the dawn breaks, sweet and clear,
The world awakes; let's spread the cheer!
For even under blankets cold,
Life's silly stories still get told.

A Hidden Canvas of Winter's Art

The snowflakes fall with grace,
Creating chaos in the race.
Snowmen with carrot noses grin,
While squirrels plot their next big win.

Painted parks, a frosty show,
Sliding kids, all set to go.
Puddles freeze, the ice will crack,
Oh, watch out for that sneaky smack!

Frosty breath, a foggy breath,
Each laugh echoes, dodging death.
Snowball fights become a sport,
While penguins wish they'd made a fort.

So let us dance on frozen dreams,
Where everything is not what seems.
With wooly hats and socks so bright,
We'll conquer winter, pure delight!

Frost-Bitten Hopes and Dreams

He wore a jacket three sizes too wide,
Tried to impress the snow with his glide.
But his skates went left, while he went right,
And down he tumbled, what a sight!

Frozen toes and noses red,
Hopes are high, but ice brings dread.
We hope to build a fort so grand,
But it melts down, just like our plan!

Laughter fills the crisp, cold air,
As we dodge snowballs without a care.
Yet under layers, we hear a squeak,
Our dreams are wobbly, so to speak!

With zip and zoom, the day goes fast,
A winter's cheer, it'll never last.
But we keep dreaming, playful schemes,
In frost-bitten hopes and dreams!

Cloaked in the Quietude of White

A blanket soft that hushes all,
Rabbits hop and deer enthrall.
But watch those footprints in the snow,
Is that a bear? Oh no, oh no!

Snowflakes tickle on our nose,
Covering trees in coats that pose.
Yet the truth hides, the world is round,
'Tis not the silence, but the sound!

With muffled giggles, secrets shared,
We tumble down, nobody cared.
In this cloak, we dance and twirl,
Who would grant a squirrel a whirl?

So raise a cup of cocoa hot,
Let's toast to friends, and laugh a lot.
In winter's white, absurdity thrives,
For within this peace, our fun derives!

Life's Pulse Within the Frozen Ground

Underneath the icy crust,
Life's little antics, oh, how we trust.
Turtles in sweaters, frogs that cheer,
Who would guess, they all come here?

The ground is hard, but vibes are bright,
As rabbits plot with all their might.
While geese quack tales, with flair and art,
They've got secrets held in every part.

Snowflakes giggle, tickle too,
Who's that dancing? Is it you?
The frozen world, a canvas spread,
Where laughter blooms, and worries shed.

So let's explore, make silly sounds,
With winter's whispers, joy abounds.
In chilly air, our spirits thrive,
There's life and fun, oh how we strive!

The Quiet Lullaby of Frost

When the world wears a frozen hat,
Squirrels slide down with a chatter and a spat.
Penguins trip over, trying their best,
While snowflakes giggle in a frosty jest.

The trees are dressed in white fluff and lace,
Snowmen have better moves in this space.
Winter laughs as hot cocoa warms the heart,
With marshmallows floating, sweet winter art.

Echoes from a Shimmering White

Footprints lead to a snowball war,
While kids laugh and tumble, craving more.
Kittens prance like they own the scene,
In a fluffy wonderland, so pristine.

The sun glints off the snowflakes bright,
Creating a disco ball of pure delight.
Even the shadows are dancing along,
In this winter circus, where all belong.

Enchanted by the Crystal Layer

Winter blankets the ground with a sneeze,
As everyone rushes for warmth with ease.
But just wait until the snow starts to fall,
Ice skating ducks will have a ball!

Frosty air makes noses red and round,
While snowballs incoming make joyful sound.
The world is a playground of giggles and squeals,
Even the frozen pond gets spinning wheels.

In the Stillness of Chilled Nights

Chill settles in like an awkward guest,
Everyone bundled up, trying their best.
Yet the moon smiles slyly with a wink,
While hot chocolate waits, as sweet as you think.

Stars twinkle like snowflakes caught in glee,
On such a night, the shadows agree.
With a wink and a nod, the winter parade,
Sends the laughter echoing, never to fade.

Enveloped in a Snowy Embrace

The snowflakes dance, oh what a sight,
They tickle my nose, give me a fright.
I slip and slide like a clumsy seal,
Wishing for boots that can truly heel.

Snowmen parade with carrot noses,
Their laughter deepens, it just cascades.
But when they melt, it's a watery mess,
Now who's got the hose? I must confess!

Echoes Lost in the White Abyss

In the silence, I hear a faint squeak,
Is it a mouse, or my sneakers that creak?
I trudge through drifts, my legs, oh so sore,
As I ponder the mysteries of winter's encore.

The trees wear coats, all fluffy and grand,
I can't help but think they just joined a band.
They swayed to the rhythm of winter's sweet tune,
While I hoped for sunshine to make an appearance soon.

Frost Kisses on Hidden Blooms

Under the blanket, life stirs and sighs,
Little flowers plot, with twinkling eyes.
They joke and giggle, beneath frosty traps,
Thinking of spring and warm, sunny naps.

A bud pats a petal, 'Don't fret, dear friend,'
'When the thaw arrives, we'll twirl and ascend.'
But for now, they're stuck, much to their dismay,
Sharing secrets of colors meant for the day!

Lingering Life, Quietly Cloaked

Inside their coats, the critters all scheme,
To throw a party, oh what a dream!
Squirrels and rabbits, with snacks laid out,
The only entrance? A very proud pout!

In whispers and giggles, they plan their grand feast,
While the world above lies still, like a beast.
But wait for the thaw, oh what a delight,
With stories and laughter beneath the moonlight!

Life's Canvas Painted White

White coats cover all the trees,
Like they're wearing winter's freeze.
Squirrels hide nuts, take a break,
Wondering if they'll wake and bake.

Snowmen dance in goofy ways,
As the sun peeks through the haze.
Frosty faces, cheeks aglow,
Taking selfies, stealing the show.

Children slip with squealy glee,
On their bottoms, wild and free.
Snowballs flying, laughter rings,
Who needs winter's serious things?

So chuckle at the chilly scene,
For winter is a silly queen.
In her realm of white delight,
We've all been kids in this frosty light.

Secrets of Sunken Roots

Roots are napping below the crust,
Holding secrets, gathering dust.
Whispers travel through the ground,
Where giggles of the past are found.

Trees gossip when no one's near,
About the critters they hold dear.
The worms are plotting mischief, too,
Oh, what a ruckus they'll brew!

Frolicking gnomes on mushroom thrones,
Share a chuckle with their bones.
Tales of yore, a jolly toad,
With every secret they unload.

So raise a cup to roots in slumber,
With tales of fun that make us wonder.
Underfoot, this laughter grows,
In the soil where nobody knows.

Nature's Quiet Dress of Ice

Nature wrapped in icy lace,
Silently joins the frosty race.
Puppies prance in frozen air,
Chasing snowflakes without a care.

Frosty crystals peek and wink,
As if they love to tease and think.
Ponds play hard to get, you see,
Reflecting mischief endlessly.

Icicles hang like sharp-edged swords,
Ready for winter's steely hordes.
But little birds just laugh and chirp,
As they dodge and make their burp.

So let us dream of chilly glee,
In frosty realms wild and free.
For laughter thrives, though cool and nice,
In this quirky world of ice.

Unseen Worlds Beneath the Surface

Oh, the critters in the ground,
Who giggle softly, never found.
Rabbits plot their escape plans,
While ants march proud with marching bands.

An underground once dull and gray,
Transforms to scenes of grand ballet.
Rats hold disco parties bright,
To keep their nights alive with light.

Worms in tuxedos glide with grace,
As snails win races at their pace.
The roots all dance, the soil sings,
In hidden worlds, they find new wings.

So here's to what we cannot see,
The laughter deep inside the spree.
In nature's party down below,
Where joy unfolds and wonders grow.

Hidden Life of the Ground

Under the chilly white blanket, they play,
Little critters dance, in a frosty ballet.
Squirrels in winter coats, strut around,
While rabbits hop, making no sound.

Beneath the icy surface, they plot and they scheme,
Digging their burrows, living the dream.
Mice in tuxedos, the party's in town,
Dancing with snowflakes, laughing, not frown.

They share inside jokes, with shivers and squeaks,
Trading funny stories, for weeks and for weeks.
But wait! What's that? A snowman looks close,
Is he watching the fun? Who's the bigger host?

With chattering teeth, they scurry to hide,
Frosty just chuckles, he's mostly outside!
So, next time it snows, don't just feel cold,
There's laughter below, in the white and the bold.

Frostbitten Secrets

Under icy cabins, secrets unfold,
Frogs in pajamas, their stories so bold.
Bunnies sip cocoa, and gossip away,
Rumors take flight on a chilly bouquet.

The owls wear spectacles, pretending to read,
While mice write a novel on how to succeed.
The trees overhear, with a gusty sway,
Laughing at critters, and their crafty play.

A snowflake's a throne for the king of the ants,
He rules with a giggle, and prances in pants.
The whispers of winter, like so many flurries,
Hide tales of mischief, in the snow that hurries.

Icicles glisten, like teeth in a grin,
As creatures below plot mischief to begin.
So if you're ever curious about what they do,
Just listen for chuckles, they're waiting for you!

A Slumbering World Unseen

Under the frost, a snoozy brigade,
With mismatched pajamas, in snowflakes arrayed.
Beavers are snoozing, with dreams of big logs,
While hedgehogs roll over like tiny old dogs.

Snowmen throw parties, with carrot cake fights,
They laugh at the chill, in their frosty delights.
The flakes twirl and giggle, they glide down with flair,
"Catch me if you can!" they swirl in the air!

The raccoons, they plot, with muffins galore,
"Let's bake in the moonlight, at the old cabin door."
But owls hoot a warning, "Keep quiet, don't shout!
Or the winter's big secret may come creeping out!"

So the world under wraps, sleeps sweetly, it seems,
In the chill of the night, they're all lost in dreams.
As snowflakes keep falling, like giggles at play,
In the hush of the evening, they frolic away.

The Weight of Winter Dreams

In the chilly air, dreams pile up high,
Little animals dream of clouds in the sky.
A porcupine's wish is a soft furry hat,
While the bear needs a nap, it's getting quite fat.

Snowflakes conspire, with whispers of cheer,
"To cover the world, let's bring winter near!"
Ducks dream of swimming, in pools filled with cheer,
But wake to discover it's frozen this year!

A moose on a skateboard dreams of a race,
He slips and he slides, then lands on his face!
The dreams of the critters, so funny and bright,
Create quite the scene in the shimmering light.

So remember this tale, when winter arrives,
That laughter and dreams keep us all feeling alive.
Dig deep in the snow, for humor unseen,
In the magical frosty, whimsical scene.

Tapestry of Frosted Secrets

The rabbit hops with such delight,

Fluffy tail showing, oh what a sight!

He burrows down but oops, he slips,

Into a pile where snowflakes drips.

The squirrel tries to leap and bound,

But lands on ice, spins round and round.

With acorns flying, what a scene,

Nature's circus, oh so keen!

The Cold Embrace of Silence

The snowman laughs with a carrot nose,

But oh dear me, where did it go?

He squints and frowns, it's all in jest,

A bird found it—who likes the best!

Frozen lakes hold secrets tight,

Skating penguins in pure delight.

They slide and dance, a wobbly show,

Chasing their tails, oh what a glow!

Beneath Winter's Gentle Hug

The snowflakes swirl in a giggly twirl,

Landing on noses, oh what a whirl!

Kids catch them here, like sticky glue,

With laughter ringing, they giggle anew.

A snowball fight erupts with glee,

But watch out! Here comes grandma's spree.

She flings a snowman like it's a sport,

And everyone dodges, 'tis quite the report!

Secrets of the Iced Ground

The ground is frozen, secrets tucked,

A sleepy bear from dreams is plucked.

He yawns and stretches, dreams in the air,

For honey, perhaps? No time to spare!

The ice is cracking, but what's that sound?

A moose on skates? Oh, how he bound!

With legs akimbo and a thud he goes,

Landing butt-first, oh how it glows!

Ghosts of the Winter Landscape

Frosty flakes twirl in the air,
Snowmen giggle without a care.
Their carrot noses are a bit whacked,
But who knew they'd become so stacked?

Squirrels buried their nuts with flair,
In hopes of finding them somewhere.
They dig and dig, but what a blunder,
They only find a pair of plunder!

A moose slips on ice in a wild prance,
Dancing awkwardly, what a chance!
With each tumble, laughter erupts,
As critters gather, all are juiced up!

Winter's ghosts in coats of white,
Make silly faces, what a sight!
As evenings come and the sun dips low,
They paint the hills with a winter glow.

Echoes Under Crystal Cover

Icicles hang like a jester's hat,
Dropping drips with a chitty chat.
Snowflakes fall, oh, what a tease,
The rooftops groan, but the trees just freeze!

Penguins waddle in a funky line,
Sliding sideways, their own design.
A snowball flies, oh, what a shock,
It hits a snowman, now he's in stock!

The moonlight glints on frozen streams,
Reflecting laughter and silly dreams.
Elves on rooftops, doing a jig,
With cups of cocoa, they all grow big!

In this winter wonder, everyone can see,
Nature's humor in harmony.
With frosty puns and chilly cheer,
We'll laugh together, season's here!

Dreams Wrapped in Ice

A polar bear snoozes, what a sight,
With dreams of fish and the moonlight.
But he rolls over and lands with a thud,
Who knew that snow could turn to mud?

Frogs in hats, hopping in glee,
Singing carols from the nearest tree.
Snowflakes jiggle to their tune,
As winter's magic spreads like a balloon.

Fluffy clouds dance across the sky,
Telling snowmen it's time to try.
But with each toss, they tumble down,
Wearing their snowcone hats like a crown!

In frosty dreams, joy we weave,
With chuckles and silliness, we believe.
This winter's fun, oh what a delight,
A playful land, shining so bright!

The Stillness of Shimmering Blankets

The yard's a canvas, pure and white,
Where kids race in like bursts of light.
They plow through drifts with a flailing zest,
Turning snowballs into a fierce quest!

A cat on the fence wears a chilly frown,
As snow falls softly, blanketing the town.
"Hey! Watch out!" she yells with a hiss,
But laughter echoes, she can't resist!

Trees wear gowns of frosty lace,
Bowing gracefully, embracing their place.
While squirrels play tag on twinkling bough,
Daring each other to show us how!

In the quiet nights, we whisper and tell,
Of frosty friends under winter's spell.
With each giggle, the snowflakes dance,
Creating joy in this snowy expanse.

Distant Silhouettes in the Snow

The snowman wobbles, looks quite round,
He misplaced his buttons, fell to the ground.
A snowball fight? Oh what a fuss!
I'm hiding here, I'm not one of us!

Footprints lead to a frosty snack,
But they're really just trails of my brother's attack.
Sleds zoom by with laughter and cheer,
Watch out! Here comes Dad, his face full of fear!

Gloves on, hat askew, oh what a sight,
Mom's laughter drowns our snowball fight.
Hot cocoa waiting, all marshmallowed bright,
But first, we'll conquer that hill of white!

The snowflakes dance like confused little flies,
We tumble and roll, oh what a surprise!
Chasing the shadows, we laugh and we play,
In the winter wonderland, until the day.

The Subtle Harmony of Frost

Jingle bells rustle, our noses turn red,
The ice cream man? No, he's hiding instead!
We build a hot chocolate turret on a whim,
Giggling as the cream starts spilling from the brim.

Time for a race, on sleds we do glide,
Watch out for the tree, or someone's backside!
Snowflakes swirl like they're having a ball,
Do winter fairies giggle as we fall?

A carrot-nosed friend stands frozen and proud,
With crooked coal eyes that say, "You're loud!"
But when the sun peeks, he'll start to melt,
Leaving us with giggles and an ice cold belt!

All bundled up with scarves and hats,
Tripping and slipping like cartoonish cats.
Snow angels flapping, looking so neat,
Winter's our playground, so frosty, so sweet!

Patterns Etched in Winter's Breath

The crunching of snow, it tickles our toes,
But I trip on a snowdrift—thankfully, no foes!
Each breath a cloud in the frosty air,
My hat's little twin is now stuck in my hair.

Sleds like rockets zoom past in a dash,
Who knew that ice would cause such a clash?
Snowflakes dive-bomb with silvery grace,
As I carve out my face in a frosty embrace.

Snow forts are castles, bring on the attack,
But really, that snowball just hit my backpack!
Huddled together, plotting our schemes,
With laughter that dances on winter's gleams.

The chill in the air cannot dampen our cheer,
Until frostbite creeps on, and then we all leer!
Hot soup and laughter resound in our heads,
Winter is funny, forget all the dreads!

The Hushed Symphony of the Cold

Whispers of frost play tricks in the night,
A squirrel's on skates? What a peculiar sight!
Snowflakes schmooze, flirting with trees,
With giggles, a little wind adds to the tease.

My cheeky dog leaps, then belly-flops down,
The snow's not deep, yet he acts like a clown.
He rolls and he tumbles, believes it's a game,
While I wipe away sneezes, feeling quite lame!

Icicles glisten, dangling like swords,
Do they know of their peril to unsuspecting hords?
Each icy drip is a prankster's delight,
As we tread lightly, silent as night.

A parade of hot drinks, marshmallows afloat,
Sprinkled with giggles, like winter's own coat.
So here's to the chill, the laughter and cheer,
In this snowy shenanigan, we'll persevere!

Winter's Silent Whisper

The chilly wind starts to tease,
While snowflakes dance with utmost ease.
A squirrel in a hat, quite absurd,
Chases its tail without a word.

In puffy coats, the children play,
Building snowmen in a funky way.
One has carrots, but he can't stand,
With a lopsided grin, he looks so grand.

Hot cocoa spills—oh what a mess!
The marshmallows float, can you guess?
A snowball flies, it hits a tree,
Then rolls back down—who's tracking me?

Under the stars, the world is bright,
Snowy cover glows in the night.
A snowman winks, is that a joke?
Or just my mind that's lost the yolk?

Secrets Held in Frost

A bunny hops with frosty toes,
Wearing a scarf that brightly glows.
He slips, he falls, oh what a sight!
Doing a dance in pure moonlight.

Icicles hang like frozen spears,
Teasing the drummers with frozen cheers.
While penguins in jackets try to skate,
And tumble down, it's quite the fate!

Mittens missing, what a plight!
A fashion faux pas in the cold night.
Yet laughter echoes down the lane,
As dogs in snowballs start their reign.

Frosty secrets flutter about,
A ice fish says, "What's that about?"
When winter chuckles, so do we,
In this frosty land of glee.

Veil of White Quietude

A quiet blanket falls from the sky,
Covering chaos with a soft sigh.
A cat in a sleigh, oh what a crew,
Chasing the moon, in a silly hue.

Old folks grumble, "Too cold to roam!"
While kids build kingdoms, far from home.
A snowball fight breaks out with glee,
As mom shouts, "Not with the dog, you see!"

With penguins waddling, they can't fall,
On slippery patches—they trip on it all.
Snowflakes giggle at the sight so grand,
As laughter echoes across the land.

Even the trees wear white hats high,
In a fashion show beneath the sky.
With each flake, a joke unfurls,
In winter's beauty, laughter twirls.

Shadows of the Frozen Earth

The shadows stretch where snowflakes land,
A frosty landscape, all carefully planned.
A moose wearing goggles stands in line,
For a snowcone topped with lemon-lime!

Snowmen gather, planning their play,
What's in the snowball? Let's just say—
The candy cane stash is quite the lure,
While snowflakes giggle, wide and pure.

Cheese in a snowball? What a tease!
A raccoon snickers, "Can I have some, please?"
As laughter blankets this frozen scene,
With silly antics that beat routine.

Beneath the veil where smiles abound,
Winter's charm seems to astound.
In every flake there's joy to be found,
In this hilarious, frosty playground.

The Winter's Breath Cradles

A snowman stands with a goofy grin,
His carrot nose is wearing thin.
With twigs for arms, he waves hello,
As chilly breezes start to blow.

Sleds fly down the hills so high,
Kids tumble down with a joyful cry.
Hot cocoa spills, marshmallows afloat,
In a cup that seems to gloat.

The penguins slide on frozen lakes,
Making friends with snowflake flakes.
A frosty dance, a silly race,
Winter's charm, a funny face!

Puffing cheeks in frosty air,
Joyful laughter everywhere.
As winter paints its frosty tale,
We giggle on this snowy trail.

Shadows of Past Lives Beneath Ice

Icicles hang like nature's fangs,
While squirrels wear the strangest bangs.
Penguins wobble with a joyful charm,
Wearing coats that keep them warm.

Footprints lead where snowmen roam,
From the park to the perfect home.
Wrapped in coats, we dance with glee,
While snowflakes twirl around the tree.

In the silent woods, a fox peeks out,
Trying not to make a sound, no doubt.
But a snowball flies and hits him square,
He runs away, with a shocked stare!

Stories whispered from the frost,
In winter's chill, we count the cost.
Yet laughter echoes through the trees,
As we embrace the winter breeze.

The Lament of Frozen Dreams

A snow globe's world, so round and bright,
With dancing figures, pure delight.
But shake it hard, watch dreams take flight,
They spin and swirl, oh what a sight!

Ice cream cones turned into frigid treats,
With every lick, a chilling feat.
Bundle up and brave the cold,
For stories of laughter will be retold.

A snowball fight, a wild affair,
With giggles echoing through the air.
Every throw meets a squeaky yell,
As we dodge and weave like a frosty spell.

Chasing rabbits in white wonderlands,
Tumbling down, we make snowman bands.
Yet in the cold, our hearts stay warm,
With laughter as winter's sweetest charm.

Echoing Silence of the Snowbound

Whispers linger in the frosty night,
As snowflakes dance, a charming sight.
A dog in boots, a snowman's friend,
Together they play, no need to pretend.

Snow angels made with flailing arms,
Giggles bright, their silly charms.
Every tumble, an echoing cheer,
New jokes to tell with every sneer.

The moonlight sparkles on the ground,
In the stillness, fun abounds.
A snowball rolls, a mischief born,
A friendly fight, winter's new dawn.

So gather round for tales of cheer,
As laughter echoes, winter draws near.
With each snowfall, our hearts ignite,
In the magic of a snowbound night.

Ephemeral Traces Under Ice

Little critters tiptoe, it's true,
Wearing socks, look at their new shoes.
The snowman winks, his eyes are bright,
Whispers secrets in the moonlight.

A snowball fight, oh, what a blast!
They throw and laugh, forgetting the past.
Fuzzy hats, all curled in grace,
Each one looks like a jolly face.

Icicles gleam like daggers of glass,
But one takes a dive and crashes fast.
The puddle laughs, it knows the score,
"Next time, buddy, just use the door!"

With frozen fingers, they try to bake,
Snowflake cookies made for the sake.
But when they taste their frosty snacks,
They turn to snowmen with silly tracks.

The Quiet Heart of Winter

Dancing flakes seem to cheekily prank,
When you catch one, it's gone—what a tank!
Sleds turn rockets, and laughter flies,
As snowy cheeks turn pink like pies.

A dog in snow suits, a curious sight,
Chasing his tail in pure delight.
"Catch me if you can!" he seems to shout,
But then he's stuck, oh no, no doubt!

Snow forts built with such regard,
Ice castles where kings dream large.
With marshmallow snowballs, all in the mix,
It's winter's aim for some wacky tricks.

As night falls softly with a yawn,
The frost-tipped moon greets the dawn.
Giggles echo as sleep takes hold,
They dream of adventures brave and bold.

Life's Keepsake in Winter's Hold

Mittens lost, a funny ol' tale,
Who knew snowmen could leave such trails?
Treasure hunts for warmth and cheer,
Finding lost scarves from last year.

Chattering teeth in the chilly air,
As snowflakes float without a care.
A snow angel with wonky wings,
Says she's ready for all fancy things.

Hot cocoa made with marshmallow fluff,
Sipping while bundled, that's the stuff!
Whipped cream battles with little kid's smiles,
They drink all day, just to have piles.

In winter's grip, where laughter rings,
A season of joy in the simplest things.
As moments freeze, they glisten bright,
In life's warm heart, a sweet delight.

The Still Breath of Dormant Ground

Pine trees dance with a glittery flair,
Whispering secrets to the frosty air.
Their branches loaded with snowy fluff,
And here we are, laughing—how tough!

A rabbit hops in a bouncy show,
Wearing a scarf, he's all aglow.
But he trips on a branch, oh dear me!
Falls in a pile, giggling with glee.

Winter winds and their playful tease,
Tickling noses like a soft breeze.
Each breath a puff, a frosty puff,
Who knew winter could be so tough?

As twilight blinks, the stars take flight,
We gather round with hearts so light.
An ice rink shines in the pale moon's kiss,
As laughter echoes—it's pure bliss.

Unseen Wonders in Frozen Depths

In the frost, a penguin slips,
With tiny flippers, it performs flips.
A snowman grins, his nose a carrot,
Lives a life quite rich, not barren.

A squirrel dances, nuts in tow,
Building castles in the snow.
While winter's chill bites at the feet,
This frosty world's dancing can't be beat.

Mysteries wrapped in icy lace,
A snowball fight in a snowy space.
Yet in this chill, laughter rings clear,
As winter plays without a fear.

And when the thaw begins the show,
Who knew beneath, joy lurked below?
With every slip and every fall,
The unseen wonders, they enthrall!

The Hidden Symphony of Cold.

The winter wind begins to hum,
A frosty tune, a frosty drum.
Noses red and cheeks aglow,
Dancing to music only they know.

A snowflake choir, each one unique,
Tickles folks' noses with every peek.
Icicles hanging, they jingle chimes,
As penguins waddle in silly rhymes.

The cold has got a quirky beat,
With snowball laughter echoing sweet.
Jumping in drifts, the world's a stage,
Winter's funk, the latest rage.

So let the cold serenade us well,
As winter's magic casts its spell.
Amid the chill and frosty delight,
Life sings on through the wintry night.

Silent Dreams of a Frozen Earth

In the hush of frost, trees wear white,
But squirrels plot their tiny heist.
Snowflakes fall like giggles from air,
Whispers of fun linger everywhere.

As bunnies hop in their soft, sleek suits,
They bounce around, both spry and cute.
A snowman's hat, a little askew,
Trying hard to be trendy too.

Under the moon, a frozen dance,
Dog paws prance, it's their winter chance.
Chasing tails in the dark so bright,
In a world where it feels just right.

Winter's calm can also tease,
With funny quirks, it aims to please.
Dreams of laughter, it stirs with grace,
In a frozen world, there's room to play.

Whispers Hidden in Winter's Grace

A fox sneaks past in a fluffy coat,
With a sly grin, he stays afloat.
Snowballs fly, a giggling spree,
In the chill, there's pure glee.

Beneath the branches, critters conspire,
Building snow forts, their hearts aspire.
The land may be frozen, but spirits thaw,
As laughter echoes in nature's jaw.

A hot cocoa smile warms the cheer,
While snowflakes play tag without fear.
In a flurry of fun, they twirl and spin,
In winter's wild dance, let joy begin!

So raise your mugs to the frosty scenes,
Cheers to the fun, the laughs, and the screams.
For in this cold, a warmth we find,
Whispers of joy in the frosty mind.

A Reverie Caught in Winter's Grasp

Snowflakes dance like tiny clowns,
They tumble down and flip around.
Winter's breath is icy cold,
But laughter shines like molten gold.

Sleds and snowballs in a race,
Face plants leave a funny trace.
Frosty noses, cheeks so red,
Giggles burst like snowflakes spread.

Hot cocoa spills, what a sight!
Marshmallow battles, oh what might!
Snowmen wear a goofy grin,
While snow angels wave us in.

So let us frolic, dance and play,
In winter wonder, joy's display.
Each sprightly laugh a snowy kiss,
In this chilly, blissful bliss!

Shadows of Life Under the Winter's Spell

Icicles dangle, nature's teeth,
Watch your step, or you'll feel the heat!
Penguins waddle with untamed pride,
While snowflakes debate who'll take a ride.

Winter hats too big, they flop,
Outdoors we tumble, fall, and hop.
A snowball here, a snowball there,
Looks like a snowman's lost his hair!

Sleds go zooming down the hills,
Cackles echo, frozen thrills.
But wait, what's that? A snow fort sprout,
Where laughter reigns, there's no doubt!

As shadows stretch and daylight fades,
We craft our dreams like frosty braids.
In frigid air, we'll spin and twirl,
Forever young in winter's whirl!

The Frosty Shroud of History

History hides in white attire,
Dusty tomes with winter's fire.
Frozen footprints tell their tales,
Of slippery mishaps—epic fails!

Snowflakes whisper secrets past,
While winter ghosts glide and cast.
Chronicles of snowy glee,
Oh, what fun those days must be!

With shovels as our trusty swords,
We battle drifts, oh, the rewards!
A snow pile here, a castle there,
Stories of triumph fill the air.

So raise a glass to icy prose,
And laugh at all the winters froze.
For even history must agree,
Winter's charm sets laughter free!

Hidden Voices in the Frozen Stillness

Under layers of chilly cheer,
Whispers linger, far and near.
Frosty jests on every breeze,
Tickling our sides with frosty tease.

Muffled giggles snowflakes keep,
As winter bears its secret leap.
What lies beneath, what tales unfold,
When cozy hearts break out and bold?

Snowman squads in stealthy night,
Plotting mischief—what a sight!
They trip and tumble, oh so sly,
With every roll, they touch the sky.

So let the wonders softly float,
In frozen dreams, we cast our vote.
For laughter jests and snowflakes dance,
In this quiet, wintry trance!

Slumbering Spirits of the Frosted Realm

In winter's chill, do spirits nap,
With frosty breath, they dream and yap.
A giggling ghost in a snowball fight,
Cackling with joy till the morning light.

Trees wear coats of white so proud,
While squirrels chuckle beneath a cloud.
They slide and glide on icy streams,
Laughing at winter's silly schemes.

Pine cones drop like snowflake bombs,
Scaring the critters with their charms.
A snowman grins with cheeky glee,
As birds chirp jokes from the old pine tree.

When frosty puffs dance in a swirl,
The rabbits wiggle, doing a twirl.
In cozy dens, all friends unite,
For funny tales by the firelight.

Whispered Tales from the Frozen Depths

Under a blanket, the earth sleeps tight,
While bugs tell stories of their fright.
A snail's slow tale brings giggles near,
As snowflakes titter and laugh with cheer.

Frogs in snow suits, what a sight!
Hopping in rhythm, trying to take flight.
They slip and slide, all in good fun,
Making snowballs, oh, how they run!

Icicles dangling like teeth so white,
The winter sun turns them in light.
A toothy grin from a frozen tree,
Shares its humor with a laugh or three.

Winds whisper secrets in chilly breath,
While shadows dance, avoiding death.
In the frozen depths, jokes come alive,
While snowmen chuckle, feeling the vibe.

The Quiet Rebirth of Nature's Soul

Hibernating bears in fuzzy dreams,
Share punchlines that make the valley beam.
With paws tucked in and noses out,
They joke about winter without a doubt.

Tucked away, the flowers snooze,
In pajamas of frost they warmly cruise.
They dream of colors, of sunshine's call,
And how to prank the first spring squall.

The grass sends whispers wrapped in frost,
Witty lines, just freshly tossed.
A root's punchline brings a chuckle fit,
As nature snickers, "Spring, we will outwit!"

As winter fades, joy will ignite,
With laughter on the breeze, a pure delight.
Tales of rebirth will bubble and rise,
In the belly of spring, where humor flies.

Echoing Lives in the Silent White

In the quiet hush, a snow fox leaps,
Chasing snowflakes as laughter creeps.
Sledding down hills with a flurry of glee,
Hollering, "Catch me! My tail's gone free!"

The snowdrifts pile, a fort's in sight,
Where kids launch laughter, snowballs in flight.
A penguin parade down the icy lane,
Tumbling about, oh what a pain!

Footprints vanish in the white glaze,
While ants play hide and seek in a daze.
Silly shadows dance on the ground,
In winter's realm, humor is found.

As the season warms, giggles will grow,
Doorways to spring will open and flow.
Echoing lives, in a joyful fight,
We welcome the sun, ending winter's night.

Dreams Entwined in Frost

Snowflakes dance on frosty air,
Chubby squirrels play without a care.
A snowman's hat, so slightly askew,
Claims he's stylish, but who knew?

Pine trees sneezing, oh what a sight,
A sprinkle of powder gives them a fright.
Icicles hanging, an artist's display,
"Watch your head!" they seem to say.

Penguins in coats, they strut around,
Waddling proudly, such joy abound.
Snowball fights turn into a mess,
Crisp laughter echoes, nothing less.

Under the frost, the world takes a nap,
While winter's antics perform their cap.
Dreams are frozen, but spirits soar high,
In the whimsical world of chilly sky.

Beneath the Glacial Embrace

Wrapped in layers, oh what a sight,
Fuzzy mittens and noses so bright.
Snowmen giggle, "We're here for the fun!",
While children tumble, joyously run.

Hot cocoa spills, marshmallows fly,
"Not on my hat!" I squeal with a sigh.
Frosty critters in chase and retreat,
Round and around on icy white feet.

Ice skating penguins, a clumsy delight,
Slip and slide, oh what a fright.
They wave hello, and tumble again,
Enjoying their winter-time frosty refrain.

In snowball battles, laughter erupts,
Pine trees giggle, all nicely dressed.
Under this cover, we're one big cheer,
Playing in winter, full of good cheer.

Shadowed Life Under Frosted Expanse

Huddled together like lost fluffy socks,
Under the stars, the moonly clocks.
Bears in pajamas and snow coats swish,
Dreaming of salmon and a warm little dish.

Icicles dripping like frozen tears,
Whispers of winter amid giggling cheers.
Skates on the lake, we glide and we trip,
With frosty breath, we laugh, and we dip.

Rabbits in scarves say, "Look at us hop!"
Chasing their tails till they tumble and flop.
Every snowflake has a giggling face,
In this frosty and whimsical space.

Under the chill, we frolic and play,
Turning winter's gloom into bright ballet.
With joy in our hearts, we dance with the breeze,
In fluffy snowflakes, we move with such ease.

The Veil of Winter's Whisper

Whispers of frost like secrets are spun,
Tickling our noses, oh what fun!
Furry little boots stomp without care,
Chasing the shadows that dance in midair.

Snowball surprise! A stealthy attack,
While laughing out loud, we all run back.
Sliding on ice, what a glorious ride,
Laughter erupts as we glide and collide.

Frogs in winter coats croak out a tune,
Making a symphony beneath the full moon.
Here comes the blizzard, but let's play a game,
In a flurry of joy, we'll learn every name.

As pine trees sway in the frosty delight,
We gather our friends for a snowman sight.
With eyes made of coal and a grin wide and spry,
Winter's embrace brings the twinkle to our eye.

Ghosts of Green Under White

The grass is under wraps, it dreams,
Of sunny days and playful beams.
But winter chuckles, sly and spry,
As snowflakes dance, oh my, oh my!

Mittens on paws, the squirrels conspire,
To find some nuts, their hearts afire.
With every slip on icy floors,
They laugh and scamper, asking for more!

In hidden nooks, the tulips pout,
While frosty breath swirls all about.
A snowman grins, with carrot nose,
He's the king of this frozen prose!

Yet when spring calls, this jest must cease,
The grass will grow, and joys increase.
But for now, let winter reign,
Ghosts of green in snowy chain!

A World Wrapped in Winter's Cloak

The world is wrapped, a quilt so tight,
With frosty patterns, oh what a sight!
Snowflakes giggle as they fall,
Each one's a prank, each one a ball.

Children bundled, looking like bears,
Tumble and roll without a care.
They build their castles, oh so grand,
While frozen mittens are in high demand!

A snowball fight erupts with cheer,
Laughing echoes, winter's premiere.
"Oh no, my hat!" a voice will shout,
With every gust, it flutters about.

But as they play in icy glee,
They know that spring will soon decree,
The cloak will fade, the chill will go,
A world transformed from white to glow!

Beneath the Shroud of Ice

Under icy drapes, we peek and grin,
At winter's show, it's time to spin.
The world tucked in, a frosty trance,
Snowmen twirl and take a chance!

The icicles hang, like chandeliers,
While penguins waddle, spreading cheers.
Wrapped in layers, not one can tell,
If I'm a snowball, or just swell!

A cozy fire, the cocoa's hot,
Marshmallows dive, oh what a plot!
While whispers of spring play hide and seek,
The snowflakes giggle, and winter's cheek!

But soon enough, the thaw will call,
We'll bring out bikes and drop the ball.
For now we dance, in icy foley,
Under the shroud, our hearts are jolly!

The Silent Heart of Winter

In winter's hush, the silence reigns,
Yet laughter bubbles in frosty veins.
A squirrel with acorns, a clumsy flirt,
Slips on ice, and oh, how he'll hurt!

The trees wear coats of shimmering white,
While winter critters plan their flight.
With every gust, they leap and bound,
They're gymnasts now on frosty ground!

Snowflakes swirl in an intricate dance,
While snowmen plot their snowy prance.
"Oh dear, my hat!" a snow-guy shouts,
As kids unleash the snowy clouts!

And though the cold may chill our toes,
It's all a game, where laughter grows.
So let us cheer, our voices clear,
In winter's heart, there's fun and cheer!

Chilled Traces of Forgotten Paths

Ice skates on puddles, what a sight,
Socks are twisted, oh, what a plight.
Snowflakes dance with a playful cheer,
They tickle my nose; winter's sneer.

Barely a trace of the path I know,
Just a slip and a tumble, oh what a show!
Laughter echoes in the frosty air,
As I chase my hat, caught in winter's snare.

Mittens mismatched, a fashion faux pas,
Yet no one cares; we're blissfully bizarre.
With snowmen grinning, they cheer me on,
While I trip on the ice, and continue to yawn.

Winter's playground, where humor's the game,
Every frosty blunder, it's all the same.
With friends all around, there's joy to be found,
In the silliness wrapped in a white wonderland.

Vestiges of Green in Wintry White

A patch of grass peeks from the mist,
Waving at snowflakes, it simply can't resist.
Squirrels slip on branches, oh what a show,
Chasing their tails in the white, they go!

The trees wear coats, so fluffy and bright,
While grass giggles softly, a comical sight.
Laughter resounds as dogs leap with glee,
Chasing those flakes, oh what a spree!

Pine cones tumble from their lofty bed,
Landing on snowmen, now with hats on their head.
"Who wore it better?" the crows seem to ask,
While clumsy little bunnies take on the task.

Amid winter's chill, there's mischief in play,
Nature's pranksters having a rollicking day.
With summer's green dreams under winter's art,
The laughter of life springs fresh from the heart.

The Crystalline Secret Beneath

What lies below this frosty sheet?
A race of tiny creatures on tiny feet?
Snowmen have secrets that they conspire,
While chuckling softly by a warm winter fire.

Awkward penguins slide with a grin,
Waddling and giggling, let the games begin!
Under their feet, a world far from dry,
Filled with sparkles and whispers as time flutters by.

Casting snowballs, we aim with glee,
Determined to hit the dog, not the tree.
But as laughter erupts at our misplaced fling,
The dog dashes back, wearing snow as a king!

So here in the chill, where fun never ends,
Each flake a giggle, as nature bends.
Under the frost, life pulses and sways,
In this frozen delight, we're lost in the plays.

Whispers of Life in Still Waters

The pond is a mirror, quite icy and bold,
Reflecting the jokes that the shadows have told.
Fish bubble up for a quick winter tease,
Flipping their fins, they do what they please.

With ducks in a row, all fluff and delight,
They quack out the tunes, a winter spotlight.
"Who needs ice skates when you can just slide?"
They giggle and waddle, what a slippery ride!

A snowy old frog takes a leap of faith,
Sinking so deep, it's love, not a wraith.
With a splash and a cheer, the giggles resound,
In the chilly embrace, joy truly abounds.

So here in the frost, life jests without care,
Garden gnomes chuckle, their secrets laid bare.
In the realm of the frozen, let the laughter ignite,
As whispers of life dance through the night.

Milton Keynes UK
Ingram Content Group UK Ltd.
UKHW022009131124
451149UK00013B/1079